WomWom stands on four
short legs. She can use her
strong legs to move and dig.

WomWom uses her legs to walk and run. She also uses her back legs to scratch.

WomWom walks slowly and she can run very fast.
Kangaroos can move quickly.
Kangaroos use their back legs to hop.

Koalas move slower than WomWom. Koalas can climb trees. Koalas use claws to hold the tree.

Galahs use their wings to fly. Galahs move their wings very fast to fly. Did you know that some birds cannot fly? The emu and the penguin have small wings so they cannot fly.

WomWom cannot run as fast as a horse. Horses can move very quickly. The horse gallops through the field.

Whales cannot fly or gallop.
Whales move by swimming.
WomWom knows whales use
their tail to swim.

Penguins are birds but they do not fly. Penguins can move on land. In the water, penguins can swim using their small wings.

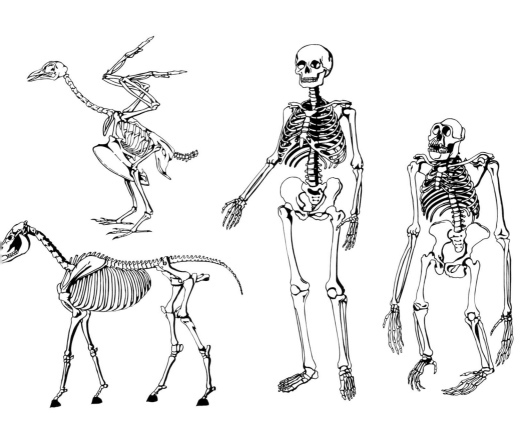

Animals have bones in their bodies. WomWom has bones in her legs to help her walk. Animals also have muscles.

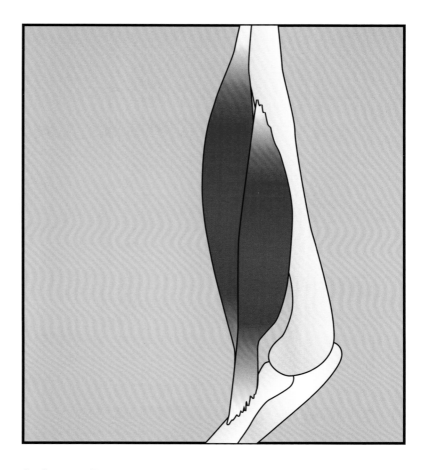

Muscles move the bones in the body. Animals can control how their muscles move. Wom Wom has strong muscles in her legs.

Did you know that
WomWom cannot fly but she
can swim? WomWom cannot
hop but she can run fast.

Animals move in different
ways. Some animals can swim
or fly. WomWom knows that
dolphins use their muscles to
swim really fast.
Some animals can hop or run.